W9-BYX-219

# Valentine's Day

Valentine's Day arrives on February 14 every year. This special holiday has come from a legend that originated in ancient times. It has been associated with the Roman feast of Lupercalia.

Today, it is considered a time to celebrate love and romance. Valentine's Day is a holiday for people of all ages. It is a time for caring and sharing. Greeting cards called "valentines" may be given and received. Sometimes gifts are bought for loved ones. Boxes of chocolate and flowers are popular items. Homemade cards and gifts are especially nice.

## Activities

Try some of these art activities for a "Hearty Art" bulletin board. First, fold an 18" (45 cm) square piece of red or white butcher paper in half. Draw a heart shape and cut out the hearts. Paint an identical pattern or design on both hearts. When dry, place the hearts together (design sides facing out), stuff with newspaper, and staple to make a heart "pillow."

Use some old magazines and cards for a collage of hearts. Cut many different sizes of hearts out of magazine pictures. Try to find pictures that have a lot of red in them or that are brightly colored. Glue the hearts in a pleasing arrangement on a 9" x 12" (23 cm x 30 cm) piece of white construction paper. Decorate between the hearts by drawing with crayon or marker or gluing pictures from old cards.

Discuss how the real heart functions and look at a diagram of a heart. During physical education, have the students check their resting pulses and then check pulses again after exercise. Talk about the importance of a warm-up activity. This would be a great opportunity to have a doctor, nutritionist, or any other qualified individual come and speak to the class. Their emphasis could be on ways to be "heart smart." Include healthy practices and the importance of nutrition and exercise.

In the math center, fill a jar with candy conversation hearts. Estimate how many hearts are in the jar. The hearts can also be grouped by tens and counted or used for some hands-on adding and subtracting. Tell the students a story problem and have them act it out with the hearts. Have students create their own problems.

Ask the students to bring in a variety of candy boxes. Use the boxes in a special "Sweet Treats" math center. Sort and classify the boxes by different categories, such as size, shape, and color. Compare and weigh them on a balance scale. Or, have students count out the correct amount of play money to "buy" a box of candy.

To learn more about the history of Valentine's Day, an excellent reference book is *Hearts, Cupids, and Red Roses* by Edna Barth. This book explores the meanings of the various symbols of the holiday, such as heart shapes, cupids, and lace.

## Bibliography

Barth, Edna. *Hearts, Cupids, and Red Roses*. Clarion, 1982.

Bulla, Clyde Robert. *Valentine Cat*. Troll, 1995.

Bunting, Eve. *The Valentine Bears*. Clarion, 1985.

Matthews, Liz. *Teeny Witch and the Perfect Valentine*. Troll, 1991.

FRANKLIN PIERCE
COLLEGE LIBRARY
RINDGE, N.H. 03461

# The Valentine Bears

**Author:** Eve Bunting

**Publisher:** Clarion, 1985

(CAN: Thomas Allen and Son; UK:
Gollancz Services; AUS: Jackaranda Wiley)

**Summary:** Mrs. Bear decides she wants to celebrate
Valentine's Day with Mr. Bear, so she sets her alarm to go
off on February 14. Mr. Bear sleeps on as she makes
signs, digs up honey, and makes a berry mix. She tries
to wake Mr. Bear, but he is not interested in getting up.
What happens next is a humorous, warm-hearted story of
two bears enjoying themselves on Valentine's Day.

**Related Holiday:** Valentine's Day is a day to recognize
the people you love. It is celebrated on February 14 in the
United States, Canada, and Europe.

**Related Poetry:** "My Valentine" by Myra Cohn Livingston, *Celebrations*
(Warren Publishing House, 1988); *It's Valentine's Day* by Jack Prelutsky
(Scholastic, 1985)

**Related Songs:** "Special Friend" and "I Get Valentines" by Patricia Coyne, *Holiday Piggyback Songs*
(Warren Publishing House, 1988)

## Connecting Activities:

- ♥ Collect stuffed bears for a special display. Give children note cards, pencils, and crayons so they
can write the names of their bears and place a card next to each bear. Or if you would like, have
them make necklace note cards. Provide yarn or string, a hole punch, notecards, and scissors so
they can hang the names of the teddy bears.

- ♥ Serve a special treat of graham crackers and honey. Try to find various types of honey, such as
clover or orange. Let children taste each type and decide what they like best and least. Make a
graph.

- ♥ Talk about fact and fiction. Ask children which this book is.

- ♥ Begin to find out more about real bears. What types of bears are there? Where do they live? As
you find out about real bears, mark a large wall map showing where they live.

- ♥ In *The Valentine Bears*, Mrs. Bear writes two poems to give to Mr. Bear. Read the poems out
loud and find the words that rhyme. Make a list of rhyming words and try using them to write
short, simple Valentine verses.

- ♥ Eat some Bears and Honey Roll-Ups. How to make them follows on the next page. Serve them
to someone special on Valentine's Day.

# Bears and Honey Roll-Ups

*Ingredients:* peanut butter, whole wheat-bread, honey, rolling pin, round toothpicks, wax paper

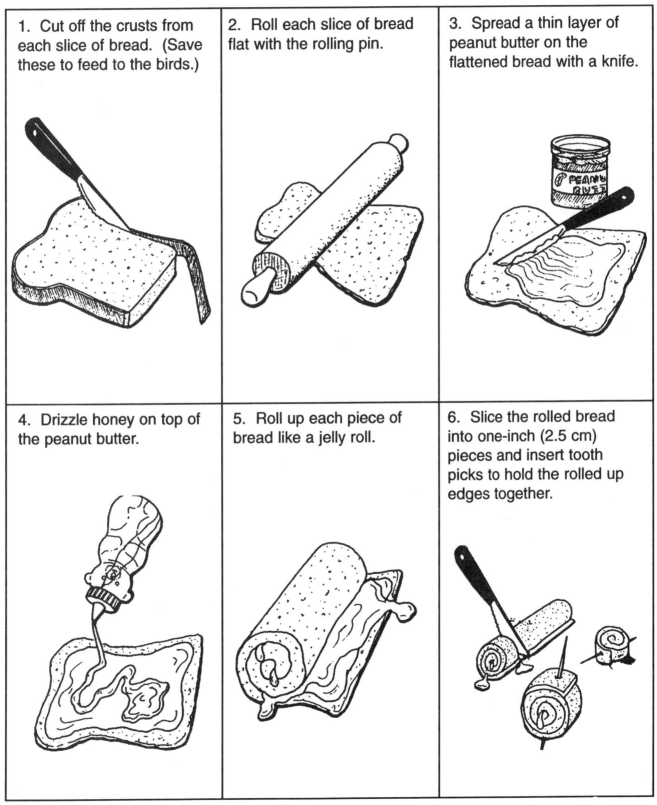

1. Cut off the crusts from each slice of bread. (Save these to feed to the birds.)

2. Roll each slice of bread flat with the rolling pin.

3. Spread a thin layer of peanut butter on the flattened bread with a knife.

4. Drizzle honey on top of the peanut butter.

5. Roll up each piece of bread like a jelly roll.

6. Slice the rolled bread into one-inch (2.5 cm) pieces and insert tooth picks to hold the rolled up edges together.

©1996 Teacher Created Materials, Inc.

# *February Bingo Game Board*

**Directions:** Copy the game board for each child. Hand out candy hearts for tokens. Use to reinforce spelling, math, science, or social studies skills.

| | | | | |
|---|---|---|---|---|
| | | | | |
| | | | | |
| | | | | |
| | | | | |
| | | | | |

©1996 Teacher Created Materials, Inc.

# Valentine Family Tree Questionnaire

Could you please help your child fill out this questionnaire about your family? We are making a Valentine family tree. Thank you!

| Mother's Side | Father's Side |
| --- | --- |
| **Mother's Full Name** *(include maiden name)* | **Father's Full Name** |
| **Grandmother's Full Name** *(include maiden name)* | **Grandmother's Full Name** *(include maiden name)* |
| **Grandfather's Full Name** | **Grandfather's Full Name** |
| **Great Grandmother's Full Name** *(include maiden name)* | **Great Grandmother's Full Name** *(include maiden name)* |
| **Great-Grandfather's Full Name** | **Great-Grandfather's Full Name** |

©1996 Teacher Created Materials, Inc.

# My Valentine Family Tree

On Valentine's Day we show our family members how much we love them. One way to do this might be to make a family tree and trace back the names of all the people who have loved you and have been loved by you.

**Preparation:** Make copies of the questionnaire on the following page and send it home with each child. When these questionnaires are returned, you are ready to start the project.

**Materials:** one piece of poster board, railroad board, oaktag, or heavy paper per child; craft sticks; blue, thin-lined markers or pens; red construction paper; colored markers or crayons; completed questionnaires

**Directions:** Tell the children that they are going to make a Valentine family tree. Give them these instructions.

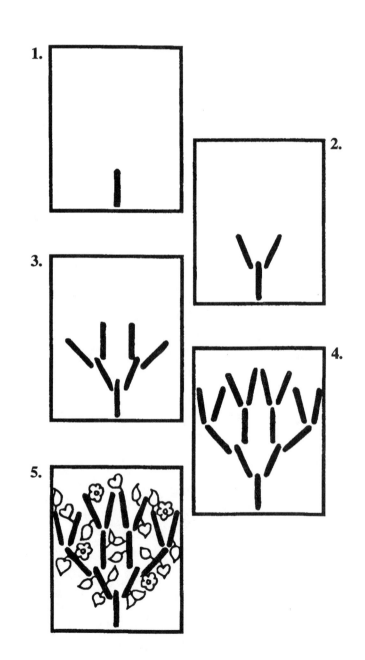

1. Write your first and last names on a craft stick. Glue this stick to the poster board to make the trunk of the tree.

2. Write your mother's maiden name and your father's name on two other sticks. Glue these sticks above the stick with your name on it. Glue them in the shape of a "Y" to make the branches.

3. Write the names of your mother's parents and your father's parents on four more sticks. Glue your mother's parents' names above your mother's name in a "Y" shape. Do the same with your father's parents' names above your father's name.

4. Do the same with your parents' grandparents. How many branches does your tree have?

5. Add leaves, fruits, hearts, and flowers, if you would like. As an extension, add the names of the family-tree-members' children to the leaves or flowers.

# Valentine Window House

**Materials:** pattern, scissors, pencil, crayons, glue, 9" x 11" (23 cm x 30 cm) plain white paper

**Directions:** Cut out the sides of the house. Cut out the windows on the dotted lines, leaving the solid line uncut so the windows and doors will open and close. This cutting can be done by pinching the paper slightly so you can make a cut with the scissors to get inside the paper and cut out the windows and doors. Glue another sheet of plain paper to the house at the edges only. Cut off the edges so that it matches the house size. On each window and the door write a word. Inside that window or door, write a word that rhymes with that word. For example, write "love" on the door and "dove" on the inside of the door. Other activities using the house include writing even numbers on the outside and odd numbers on the inside or an equation on the outside and the answer on the inside.

©1996 Teacher Created Materials, Inc.

# *Mystery Picture Directions*

In order to complete the Valentine mystery picture explain the directions on this page to the children, then reproduce only the color key and the coloring directions. Give each child a blank graph sheet and a copy of the directions. Make sure not to reproduce the answer key picture. If the directions read: Color R/PK A6, C11, F2, the children follow up line A and across line 6 with his or her fingers until they meet on square A6. Then they color that square half and half as indicated on the color key. The children do the same to squares C11 and F2. They should cross out each letter-number as they work on it.

```
                    Color Key

   LG = Light Green        PK = Pink

   R = Red                 PL = Purple
```

Color PK/LG G5 H6

Color LG G4 E6 B5 A10 D11 C7

Color PL E3 C1 A1 D1

Color R C9 E11 G10 F4

Color LG E7 D8 H10 F2 A4 A6

Color PK\R E10 F9 PL\LG H3 B8

Color PK E4 G7 LG\PK E8

Color LG D6 B11 H8 F11

Color R D9 G11 C3 E5 C10

Color LG D2 A5 B3 H9

Color LG F1 H5 A2 B6 A11 H11

Color R D3 C11 D5 C5

Color PK F8 G6 E9

Color LG F10 B9 D7 B2

Color LG\PK F7 LG\PK F6 PL\LG H2 B7

Color LG C8 G1 D10 H4 C2 A9

Color PK/LG G8 H7 LG/PL A7 A8 G2 G3

Color PL E1 E2 B1

Color LG H1 B4 C6 D4 A3 B10

Color R G9 F5 C4 F3

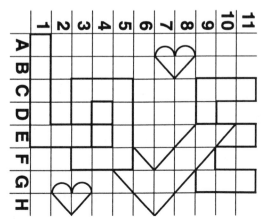

# Mystery Picture

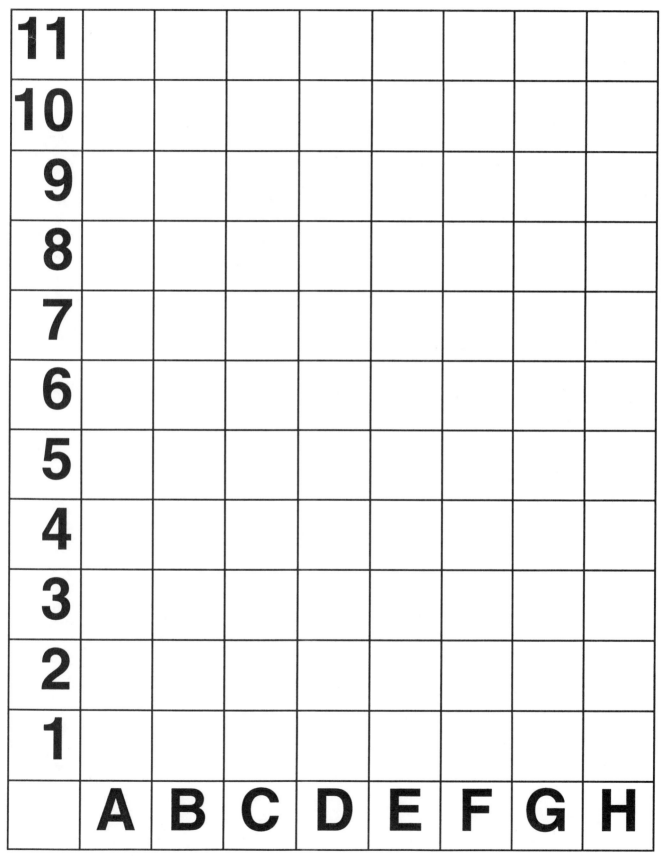

# Valentine Card

Follow these directions to make a special Valentine card.

**Materials:**

- 2 sheets 8 ½" x 11" (22 cm x 28 cm) white construction paper
- 1 sheet 8 ½" x 11" (22 cm x 28 cm) pink construction paper
- 1 8 ½" x 11" (22 cm x 28 cm) red construction paper
- Variety of other colors of construction paper
- Crayons or markers
- Scissors
- Glue

**Directions:** As each pattern on the following pages indicates reproduce or trace onto construction paper. Then follow the steps on this page to create a Valentine card, using the clip art on the last page to decorate the card. Write a message to someone special in the center of the card. As a variation use a large, round doily instead of white construction paper for the background.

- Step 1 - Glue the red heart onto the white construction paper.
- Step 2 - Glue the pink heart onto the red heart.
- Step 3 - Glue the white heart onto the pink heart.
- Step 4 - Decorate with clip art and write a message to someone special.

©1996 Teacher Created Materials, Inc.

Reproduce onto heavy red paper.

Reproduce onto heavy pink paper.

Reproduce onto heavy red paper.

Use this clip art to decorate cards.

# Unique Valentines

## This Is Your Life

**Materials:** magazines, 18" x 24" (46 cm x 61 cm) construction paper, glue, scissors, scraps and notions for decoration

**Directions:** Think about the people to whom you want to give these Valentines. What do they like to do? What foods do they like to eat? What music do they like? Do you have any photographs of them? Look through the magazines and cut out anything that reminds you of the people for whom you are making the gifts. Arrange everything on the construction paper. Make it look as nice as possible. Glue it down. Add bits of ribbon, paper hearts, doilies, etc. Write a special poem or note and glue it on the paper. This will be a very special gift.

## Heart Links

**Materials:** pink and red construction paper, heart patterns below

**Directions:** Give each student one sheet of pink hearts and one sheet of red hearts. Have them cut out the hearts. Then, have them cut out the center of the hearts by cutting through the bottom one. Link the hearts together (red-pink-red-pink) then tape the bottom of the heart back together. Use them to decorate the classroom.

## Healthy Heart Collage

**Materials:** magazines or newspapers, construction paper, glue, scissors

**Directions:** Cut out pictures of heart healthful food from the magazines or newspapers. Hide some pictures in the collage that would not be good for your heart. Trade papers with a friend. Can your friend find the pictures that are not heart healthy?

**Variation:** Write the names of the foods on or below the pictures and a yes if they are healthy and a no if they are not.

# A Puzzling Message

Write your own Valentine message on the puzzle below. Then, cut out the pieces on the dashed lines and place them in an envelope that you have addressed to that "special person." You can write a message to your best friend, a favorite relative, or your teacher. Watch your valentine have fun putting the puzzle pieces together!

©1996 Teacher Created Materials, Inc.

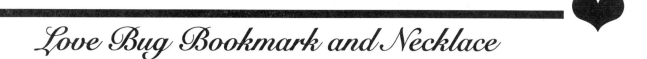

# *Love Bug Bookmark and Necklace*

Children can make these special gifts to express their love to those who are dear to them.

**Materials:**

32" (82 cm) piece of red yarn, red and white colored paper, small picture of student, scissors, glue, crayons

**Directions**

1. Cut out two red and two white hearts.

2. Glue the picture of the student onto one white heart. Write "I Love You" on the other white heart.

3. Color two red hearts to look like "love bugs."

4. Spread glue onto the back of one red and one white heart.

5. Sandwich one end of red yarn between the two hearts.

6. Repeat with the two remaining hearts on the other end of the yarn. Let dry.

FRANKLIN PIERCE COLLEGE LIBRARY

00101529